Praise for Daniel W. Wright:

"Dan Wright's *Brian Epstein Died for You* is the evolution of the artist as a young man. In it, Wright explores the drunken moonlight of St. Louis nights, his own struggle to just get by, and just exactly how it is he came to be here. This is a collection that offers no easy answers, much like life itself."

-John Dorsey, Author of *Your Daughter's Country*

"Daniel W. Wright is one thing that's rare these days— a true original. His work connects on all the right levels and you will never be let down when you see his name on a cover. *Brian Epstein Died for You* is a book that, from start to finish, will stay with you and is a must for any true fan of great poetry."

-John Patrick Robbins, Editor-in-Chief of the
Rye Whiskey Review.

Praise for Daniel W. Wright:

"Daniel W. Wright crafts his poems with a sort of hypnotic irreverence. He is not concerned with artifice and posturing. Rather, he uses blunt, clipped language to tell his readers about the world underneath the glass—the world we might inhabit if we put our mirrors down long enough to look one another in the eyes. When he writes: *I get sick of people talking about ALMOST/ as though ALMOST is a victory,'* we understand that the poems in this new collection are a call to action, a cry to be seen as individuals divorced from personality, politics, and victimhood. Wright is a poet of the everyman, yes, but he is also a poet of the human animal who longs so ferociously for connection that we have no choice but to pause, to say *look closer,* and maybe, just maybe, slow down and honor the best in ourselves and each other."

-Kelli Allen, Author of *Banjo's Inside Coyote*

Brian Epstein Died For You

Poems by Daniel W. Wright

Kansas City   Spartan Press   Missouri

Spartan Press
Kansas City, Missouri
spartanpresskc.com

Copyright © Daniel W. Wright, 2020
First Edition1 3 5 7 9 10 8 6 4 2
ISBN: 978-1-950380-90-9
LCCN: 2020932144

Design, edits and layout: Jason Ryberg
Cover image: Gabrielle Blanton
Title page image: Brandon Barnes
Author photo: James Wilkinson
All rights reserved. No part of this publication may be reproduced or transmitted in any form or by any means, electronic or mechanical, including photocopying, recording or by info retrieval system, without prior written permission from the author.

The author wishes to acknowledge the following poets, people, and places:

To Neeli Cherkovski, thanks for showing me the great poets. To Kevin Ridgeway, one of the best poets in Los Angeles. Glad I got to visit Hank's grave with you. To the Beat Museum, thanks for making me feel at home. To Niko Van Dyke, Anthony Buchanan, Brandon Loberg, and Charlie Getter. That reading was probably one of the most of fun I've had in a while. To Jason Baldinger, it's been an honor to share the road and the stage with you as often as I have. To Livery Company, always a home away from home. To Denmark Laine, the founder of the American Paranoid Society. I can't think of a better partner in crime. To Alana Harmon, my sister from another mister. Thanks for keeping my dumb ass in line. To Jeanette Powers, thank you for always being an inspiration and for letting me sleep on your couch. To K.W. Peery, Shawn Pavey, and Brandon Whitehead, you all make Kansas City so much fun. I hope to be as good of a poet as you all are someday. To Prospero's Books and Dunaway Books, it's the great used bookstores of the world that make writers feel welcome. To every other poet I've had the pleasure of reading with this past year, I hope to see you all again down the road. To Spartan Press for believing enough in my work that there's more than one of these now. Finally, to the readers, thanks so much for picking up *Rodeo of the Soul* and my early chapbooks. I hope you all like this one as well.

TABLE OF CONTENTS

Painting While Cycling with Picasso / 1

Well Shit... / 3

A Few Words for Michael Castro / 4

The Regular / 5

On a Bus in Los Angeles / 7

Two Streets / 8

Almost / 10

Rodeo of the Soul II / 11

The Only Thing I'm Sure of is Beer / 14

Becky Lynch Took Steve Austin to Dick Kick City / 16

Nostalgia's for the Birds / 18

California Feelin' / 19

Tentative Platform for the Presidency
    of Keith Richards / 21

No Shame in This Walk / 23

Attack of the Killer Books / 25

That Dylan Moment / 29

Cookbooks Are Just Action Figures for Grown-Ups / 30

A Matter of Measurements / 32

Castle / 34

Crop Circles Are Gone, Big Foot is Dead / 36

Thursday Rain / 38

Red Flags / 40

Heart to Hart / 41

Gatekeepers / 43

Blacktop / 45

Your Latest Local Music Darlings / 46

Slingshot / 48

With This Cigarette, I Thee Wed / 49

Quick Thought #4,000,097 / 51

Rodeo of the Soul III / 52

WHATEVER happens tomorrow, one thing is certain; it must not be allowed to look after itself.

-Brian Epstein, *A Cellarful of Noise*

Painting While Cycling with Picasso

Greet all I see
with *Good evening
friends and enemies*
because it's just
as politically correct
as it is truthful

Annoyances only ride coattails
claiming they're feuding with you
while you don't really know
who they are

I want to ask the next woman
that comes into my life
who wants to describe herself
as *a little quirky*
to please go away
before things get bad
for the both of us

Had a friend spend all my money
he said it was for a good cause
He had no beer at his house
had no money on him either
He blamed that on the law

I don't know when
but one day I woke up
and my life became
a bunch of Willie Nelson songs

Drinking wine under mid-west stars
searching for what you consider
to be peace
Wiping your nose so much
from illness and allergies
people don't know
if it's the weather
or if you have a coke problem
With weather as bipolar
as half of your friends,
even your immune system
says *Fuck it!*

Making dinner at ungodly hours
because no one
should go to bed
hungry
It may only be Ramen
but dammit it's still something

What some call excuses
others call experience
Don't ask me a thing
I might tell you the truth

Well Shit…

Somebody committed suicide today
so I didn't have to
and somebody else got close
but chickened out at the last second
For most people
the closer you get to death
the more you appreciate life
Maybe then
more politicians
need a healthy dose
of near-death

I hope I can find the person who chickened out
and buy them a beer or a hamburger
I'll try to make them laugh
and then we can toast
to the one
who did die today

A Few Words for Michael Castro

Reading your work on Christmas Eve
in a Tower Grove pavilion
from a book borrowed from RDW
Wishing I could've known you better
but grateful for opportunities
of pleasant conversations we did have

Always listened when you spoke
because there was always something to be learned
Always looked like a prophet when I saw you
felt unworthy to say hello first few times
Imposter syndrome
turned to eleven
when you meet those
you respect from afar

Didn't they give him a sword for his poetry? Denmark asks
Close. I replied *They made him poet laureate.*
Truth is all anybody can ask for
Thank you for yours

I'll end this poem by saying to you on paper
what I said last time I saw you
Thanks for leading the charge
Rest in peace
Good sir

The Regular

She sits at the end of the bar
Twenty-two years old
Been a regular since she was seventeen
Two abortions and another she gave up for adoption
for a boyfriend who wound up
not giving her
the happily ever after
he promised

Once empathic but now embittered
she shoos away
any chance of a good life
because things never went
as planned
Rumors are facts and facts are hearsay
depending on if she likes you

A search for love
that never extends beyond a shot
She's been with enough guys
who've come and gone
learning to just get over being hurt
because they certainly did

She looks older than she is
Forced to be a Mother Hen
to those lucky enough
to be irresponsible
Nothing ever changes for her
And that's how
she likes it

On a Bus in Los Angeles

Actress talks to the bus driver
her accent going back and forth
between a Minnesota housewife
and Rosie Perez
Turning a story about a shitty boss
into a speech
about American freedom

Pictures of jean models
keep sleeping bums company
I want to support
the American worker
but how can I
when a machine pays better attention
to simple details

Two Streets

Jim walked home
after the bar charged him
full price for a beer
because he hadn't realized
that happy hour was over
Y'know, it really is a shame
that happiness can only last for an hour he drunkenly bemused
Actually, happy hour lasts for about four hours said the bartender
And a wonderfully long hour it's been replied Jim

He stumbled his way home,
enjoying a St. Louis evening
in the springtime
He made the turn
onto a street
that looked like his street
and kept track of the numbers of the houses
until he reached the number
that should have been his
Only something was wrong
The number was correct
only the house
looked different

Jim lived with his friend
on the upper floor

of a two-story flat
that had once been a mansion
Yet now it seemed to have transformed
into a house
shaped like a square
and made almost entirely of stone
Jim cautiously stepped up to the door
and knocked on it.
A man in an undershirt
and gym shorts
answered the door
Is this 4752 Botany Way?
No. said the man,
obviously pissed
at having his life interrupted
by a drunk
This is 4752 Erwin. Botany is two streets down.

Jim looked around confused
Are you sure?
The man slammed the door in Jim's face
and yelled from the other side of it
that he would threaten
to call the cops
Hey! said Jim *You wanna know something,*
I may be drunk
but tomorrow morning I'll be sober
and you'll still be an asshole!

Almost

I get sick of people talking about ALMOST
as though ALMOST is a victory
I almost asked them out.
I almost got that promotion.
I almost went to that show.

Okay

Well, I almost just scratched my balls
a few minutes ago
but I didn't
and they still itch

Rodeo of the Soul II

Two years is a long eight seconds
Garden grows
Don't ask the same question too many times
The rich get richer and the poor get prison
There's much more beyond the sea of reality
Ghosts of revolutionaries haunt
the silence of modern worlds

I don't know what to do with a God
Take it away before it scares me
Winds rev themselves up
to be so cold they burn
Education leaves San Francisco
as starving artists
struggle through winter
without four walls
Buena Vista Park bohemians
ready to kill for an ounce

Early morning anxieties
remind you that being working class
these days
only means that you're poor
but don't do meth
Don't care about being rich
just don't wanna be poor

Drinking in Whitman's chair
underneath Brooklyn Bridge
Artistic entitlement
entangles half-wit writers
in their own mess
Last lessons to unlearn
Freedom isn't always what you want

Mickey Mouse motorboats Marilyn Monroe
as Medusa Madonna eats McDonald's
Yin Yang Charlie Brown eats Chinese food and Donuts
Empty bottles are the church bells
of that which is unfulfilled
God points an American made gun
at Adam

Psychedelic tantrums no longer progressive
Sitar-spangled banner
brings rain to wash reality
to cover the earth with new dew
Death masks lie in wait
within the eye of silence
Tree trunk coffin for lovers
Nothing closer to the spiritual plane
than music
pure and easy
Carve out a book and call it home

Those who look to the stars
are never alone

Too tight to incinerate
Mirror only reflects curves
Choir forsaken Christ mystic
lonely for the archetypal archangels
to shape the world
Kingdom defeats diffusion
speaks in riddles to communicate
Faces reflect in Rorschach slides
Closed eyes put head in the sand
Just be a big boy,
it'll all be over soon

Face to face with dead eyes
on the battlefield
where the moon says
I love you
Exhausted dreams
lose place in countdowns
Kick the bottle
Watch it skid
Success has many fathers
but failure's an orphan

The Only Thing I'm Sure of is Beer

I sat in the living room
in emotional shock
when I heard how my girlfriend
talked to her family
when she was under stress

She had talked to me like that
the weekend before
making me feel
like a kid
who was always a disappointment
As usual
I wondered if I'd been thoughtless
and fucked up
I'm used to fucking up

But after we got home
She acted as though
everything was suddenly fine
and I began to think
I had imagined
the whole damn thing

My hands couldn't hold on
to an emotion

so,
I sat in the living room
while my girlfriend
fixed up her new bedroom
When her mother walked by later
and asked if I wanted a beer
I said *yes*

It was the only thing I knew for sure

Becky Lynch Took Steve Austin to Dick Kick City

Butcherknife
for a slow day
All beliefs
should be left
in the church pew
Handcuffs never enough
to stop desire

Hard work beats talent
when talent doesn't work hard
provided you pay upfront
Determination
is more
than the body

You gotta be cruel
to be careless
Never underestimate
a desperate soul
because they have
nothing left to lose

Being called
the next previously big thing
is an insult

to those who work hard
to be recognized
as the bonds of yesteryear
can never hold the present
How can anything ever stand on its own
When comparison
is always too easy

Nostalgia's for the Birds

I held a party for old friends
after I ran into them,
catching up on our lives
And we all thought
we should have one last get together
for old time's sake

Somehow, it all came down to me
As it often does
to put everything together
I sent out messages
asking everyone
how their schedules looked

We all agreed on a date
and everyone seemed excited
until the day of the party.
It was nice to see
the few who did show up
but it confirmed
what I already knew
deep down
Nostalgia's a mirage
You can't swim in it
but you can definitely drown in it

California Feelin'

Sunset Boulevard hopefuls
all want discovery
Let the ocean
wash them all away

Smoke splits blue sky
Gatsby eyes look down
A million different kinds of music
blend together
as a million languages laugh
with each other

Books passed like peace pipes
to sidewalk squatters
Don't you understand?
We've found the main nerve!

Sundresses in winter
dance to what remains
of free love
Puppers only want to cuddle
No one understands
unconditional love
like dogs

Falling for flapper hat wearing
hipster pixie dream girls
that seem to be everywhere
Typing away on Apple computers
drinking tea

whilst I drink a mocha
I could swear
is actually
just heated chocolate milk

The restless and derivative
sell themselves
and the Great American script
in elevators
to anybody wearing a blazer
with a decent haircut

Sunshine states don't know
what to do with themselves
when the sun goes down
Tired tears prep second wind
Daily grind soundtracks in mono
like a one-track mind

California vibrations grow the world
Drink yourself drunk at Vesuvio
and stumble down Jack Kerouac Way
Empathic hearts take blame
and kiss with kindness
all the same

Without love
the world is just another place

Tentative Platform for the Presidency of Keith Richards

1 - The official slogan for my campaign shall be *I've Upped My Standards. Now, Up Yours.*

2 - Re-instating the right to smoke in bars any time the weather is below 45 degrees.

3 - A Beatle must be left open to the same level of legal and judicial scrutiny as a Rolling Stone.

4 - Moving Black History Month to a month with at least 30 days and some decent weather.

4A - Instituting a Woman's History Month, also in a month with at least thirty days and some decent weather.

5 - Free health care for all, no strings attached. For every month this is not instituted during my presidency, a cut in the defense budget shall be made.

6 - No law concerning drug enforcement shall be voted on by those who have financial interests in pharmaceutical companies.

7 - The birthdays of Ron Wood and Bobby Keys shall be considered national holidays.

8 - The Queen, as lovely as she may be, can kiss my majestic Satanic arse.

9 - Instead of being treated as criminals, heroin addicts should be treated by health care officials in an environment where they can have a real chance to get better.

10 - Cracking down on the music companies and online streaming services who keep the money for themselves and instead make sure the artists get a fair deal.

11 - At least once during the first term, Mick Jagger must publicly lick my undercarriage in an act of humility.

12 - The new poet laureate of America shall be Tom Waits.

13 - For every child shot in a school shooting, a member of the legislative branch shall be shot as well. Nothing serious, but enough to give them an idea to actually do something.

14 - Putting money into public education in order to create a well-informed electorate.

15 - Instituting a Green New Deal and dedicating time and money to finding alternative solutions and greener options in order to cut down carbon emissions, including government-paid job training for greener options for those who work in the energy industry.

16 - Finally, it will be the opinion of this administration that if you don't know the blues, you shouldn't pick up a guitar.

No Shame in This Walk

Strolling your happy ass home
after spending the night
peering in the windows
of neon-lit bars
to see if you can find familiar faces
that'll convince you
that bad habits
are a good idea

Only options are a bed
you pay the rent for
or a late-night diner
that's cash only with no ATM
and you decide to go to bed
because sleep is better
than a convenience charge
along the way

Police sirens in the distance
let you wonder
if they're going for your friends
who were too drunk to drive
but insisted they could handle it
because they've driven home
in worse states before

and you're glad
that you're close enough to you place
to walk
because you know
they would've busted
your ass first

Attack of the Killer Books

Once upon a time
books were read everywhere
They inspired ideas
and brought about conversations
There was always a book to be read
or a book to be shared
and the books felt happy
to help the humans understand
each other
a little bit more

Then one day,
the books stopped being read
The humans suddenly preferred
shiny objects of all sorts
and the books began to feel lonely
They huddled together on shelves
to keep each other company
but couldn't help but observe
people start to resent each other more
and see education fall
and see the rise
of people taking pride
in anti-intellectualism

So
one day,
the books decided
to do something about it
They opened the windows of the libraries,
the bookstores,
and the apartments of the world
Deciding to kamikaze themselves
in the name of killing
the anti-intellectuals

All across the world
police were baffled
as more and more town idiots
found themselves
with their heads caved in
and a book right beside them
and all shiny objects cast to the streets
to be run over by cars
that didn't see them
One case even had a man's blood
and brain matter
spell out
SPLAT
along the sidewalk
just in case people didn't realize
what had happened to him

As the phenomenon grew,
conspiracy theories began to spread
Some blamed the Illuminati
some blamed the Free Masons
some even blamed Elvis
but there was little evidence
to support that theory

The police began to look
at security footage
to see if there were any clues
but there were none
The books were too smart
People began to be
so scared for their lives
that they began to start carrying books around
so that whoever was killing these dumbasses
wouldn't target them
They walked with books in their hand
had books beside them at bars
and eventually
began reading these books
Soon the murders stopped
and intelligence began to rise again
and like all things
The Dunce Deaths
which was later changed to
The Moron Murders
until finally it was called

*The Spree of Fatal Incidents Involving Those
Who Would Be Classified as the Educationally
Disenfranchised*
(so as to not risk offending anyone)
faded into memory

But the books knew
that eventually
another shiny object
would come around
to distract people from reading
And whenever that next shiny object
showed itself
the books would be ready

That Dylan Moment

The drunk never stood a chance
as he tried to get sober
The usual crowd cajoled him
and bought him rounds
trying to get him
to be his former self
what they called
his usual self
as it dawned on him
in that Dylan moment
that they preferred him
in two dimensions
instead of three

When they got him
three sheets to the wind
they began to point
and laugh at him
as they always had before
That was something
they could understand

Cookbooks Are Just Action Figures for Grown-Ups

Weight gained
New freckles too
Body begins to ache with the weather
though my eyes
are ever the same
Lines that weren't there before
more noise when I stand up
and a little more grey in my hair
though I'm excited about that

The same people
I used to drool over toys with
now just drool
over cookbooks
I guess cookbooks
are just action figures
for grown-ups

Don't know how much of my life
has passed
I love the uncertainty
of not comparing myself
to others anymore
even if bad habits are still
hard to break
sometimes

Once thought
I'd have a wife and kids
Once had a wife
didn't work out
No one to settle with
because settling in life
means giving up
Can't run
as hard as I used to
Just enjoying the view
until it's time to go

A Matter of Measurements

Just another
one-sided dick swinging contest
for a Duckie
who finally got his Andie
Giving every guy
your girlfriend hugs
the stink eye

Sticking your nose
into personal conversations
you have no part in
only because
your girlfriend is a part of it
Making sure
her every male friend knows
you're there

You don't need to worry
we're not like you
Who waited so patiently
for what you felt
you deserved
Every last one of us
have our own lives

So don't worry
none of us will try
to break the two of you up
You're doing
just fine
on your own

Castle

All I can remember
is looking up
because that's what I had to do
to see everything
An apartment building
that looked like a castle
with a courtyard
and a gate to keep
invading forces at bay

My mother's smile
as I pretended to be the wrestlers
I saw on tv
Riding a big wheel
with peddles that moved all the time
but a wheel
that only moved some of the time

Chicago always seemed cloudy
But a kid never cares about the weather
Only where their imagination can go
at the moment
Eating Cheerios out of plastic bowls
that were '70s yellow
The backs of apartments
seemed like jungle gyms
begging to be climbed

The tall buildings felt
like a warm blanket
as we walked along the streets
and I never wanted
anything more

Crop Circles Are Gone, Big Foot is Dead

Everyone wants to tell me
the conspiracy theories that they believe in
Wild-eyed and varied
Yet when I share
the one conspiracy theory
I full-heartedly believe in
That Courtney Love had a hand
in the death of Kurt Cobain
that's apparently too much
for some people to handle

The FBI had a hand in the deaths
of JFK, RFK, MLK, John Lennon, and Jesus?
Dude, it goes back to the Knights Templar!
9/11 was an inside job?
Look at what W does with his pinky finger
at the school when he found out!
It's a signal to his brothers in Skull and Bones!
The aliens landed at Roswell?
You gotta look hard at the footage but it's there!
Bill Hicks faked his death and became Alex Jones?
Dude, look at some old Bill Hicks bits! He was alt-right
   before alt-right!
The idea that the Mandella effect
is just the experiencing of the multiverse?

I swear Berenstain used to be spelled differently!
And I say fine
Believe what you want to believe
That's the beauty of humanity
Just don't necessarily dismiss
the idea of a junkie
that had been caught cheating
on her rock star husband
who didn't want that gravy train to leave
and thus had a hand in his assignation
to collect on insurance, royalty checks, and his legacy
I guess that's too out there for some

Beliefs are a funny thing

Thursday Rain

Without fail
it rains every Thursday
It's been doing this
the past few years
and I can tell you
my shoes aren't made for this
They get soaked
in a matter of seconds

The last few storms
have brought out
toads on the sidewalks
as henchman breezes
take out umbrellas
leaving people
to run to safety
or to huddle with themselves
on a long walk home

Everyone has their reasons
for why they think
it's like this
I don't care which reason is true
though I have my suspicions

I just want the sun
to stay a full week
without the clouds
getting in the way
of a good time

Red Flags

I'm always the one
accused of being immature
and not knowing how a relationship
is *supposed to work*
Some older men
always want to say
Happy wife, happy life!
like that's some sort
of sage-like advice
and call me a fool
when I call bullshit

No one ever asks
what I believe in
I'm just an accessory
in my own relationship
People ask why I always
want to point out red flags
I tell them
*If you pay attention
to warning signs on the road,
why not pay attention
to the ones in your heart?*

That's when they say
that I know nothing

Heart to Hart

Burned the bridge
that the rest of us were on
Another needle with the damage done
You're not allowed to come around
to the bar
I love you like a brother
but only from afar
I won't acknowledge you
while they're nearby
and I won't be made a fool again
by believing that they're gone

I don't know what you believe
As soon as I do,
I'll know what I believe
Everyday gossips cloud matters of fact
Sometimes I wish it was 2015
so all of us could sit at a table
like we used to

I wrote you a few eulogies
when I thought you might die
Glad you beat the cancer
that took your eye
but that doesn't mean

a friendship is fixed
I hope one day
things can be better
I hope one day
we can all hang out
like we used to

Gatekeepers

They don't want you
unless you got money to give them
and a degree to brag about
They don't care about your truth
as long as you look good
in your author bio
They won't care what you do with your life
unless it involves you telling the world
how they are more woke
than you will ever be

Progressive magazines never want
the poor poet who has seen more
than they'll ever know
Who came to art as a desperate last grasp
to yell at the world without going to jail
Who may have even been behind bars
a time or two
and still kept a good head
on their shoulders

They will only be dismissive
because they don't understand
the true pain of doing everything right
only to still fail

So, they sweep the world's pain under the rug
like everything else
then wonder why incidents like Ferguson
ever happen
They'll wear a Black Lives Matter shirt
just because it makes them look
like they're on the right side of history
but in truth
they're too scared to ever attend a protest
They will hide when the war
comes to their front door
They will claim to be above so much
yet stand for so little

They'll mind the gates
to say what they do matters
only so no one figures out
They were never needed
in the first place

Blacktop

I was the kid
on the blacktop
with nowhere to go
Made fun of
for being too stupid
in class
because I preferred
to be in my imagination
and for knowing things
nobody else cared about

Walking along the fence
enjoying the moments
no one wanted
to mess with me
Each second felt precious
before the bell rang
and it was time to go in
and learn things
I was too scared
to care about

Your Latest Local Music Darlings

Looking like second-rate caricatures
in a fourth-rate song
The band only wants
to keep the party going
Living stereotypes
long past their prime
Going through motions
like they go through women
who stay the same age
so they won't ever be smart enough
to see them as they are
because no woman their age
would deal with them.

They never tour
because they never want to sell out
and barely promote their shows
with promoters screaming at them
saying *Don't you know*
Brian Epstein died for you!
They'll always lose steam
after the first release
that first and only true burst
of creativity
Winning fixed polls
in whatever local music magazine

When you ask them their influences
they'll always mention
Dylan or the Beatles
to show you
they mean business

Losing jobs and losing gigs
blaming everything on the scene
that already accepted them
Drink the money they made in a night
because it's never enough
though not their fault
Talking shit like a sowing circle
about every other band
who they'll always support
and who they know
got their backs

Breaking up before breaking through
but just you wait,
the new projects of the main songwriters
THAT is gonna be the one
that'll make it big time.
Just you wait and see!

Slingshot

Woke up
from licking my wounds in booze
It doesn't matter
what the bigger picture is
Sometimes you just need
to feel sorry for yourself
and be pissed at everything
for a day
without any words of wisdom
that only make you want
to punch the mouth
they're coming from

Not everyone wants their life
to be a slingshot
To take twelve steps back
to get twenty steps ahead
Some say that you sometimes
gotta go through Hell
to get to Heaven
That may be
but I'd still prefer the direct route

With This Cigarette, I Thee Wed
A Poem for Josh and Whitney Eaker

Soul mates are truly
a rare thing in this world
and they don't always come
in ways we expect
Some come as best friends
Some come as family
Some come as lovers

Not many in this world truly deserve
happily ever after
as much as they think they do
But its those who give everything
they have
for their friends
who can find it
as you both have

Blessed be the ones
who love only because
their hearts know honesty
from the great lie
Failure can happen
but always know
you can get back up together

Nothing stops a united front
You will always have love
and that is the best comfort
one can have
Forever with kindness and empathy
and a friendly *Hail Satan!*

Quick Thought #4,000,097

I'll just go ahead
and say it
White people scare me
when *Sweet Caroline*
comes on

Rodeo of the Soul III

Psychedelia was a fad
buy it wholesale
People want drugs
and they'll love you
if you're an upper
Dreamachine demon smiles
like a Juggalo jester
Secret sixties songs
only a moment to enjoy
and another dragon to chase

River De Peres overflows Carondelet
like an Eliot poem
with tar and oil flowing in the water
down the streets
That was never the Thames
it was always the Mississippi
Humans splash in the filth
and dogs keep away from it
Mosquitoes caught in the act
leave blood on your hands
Bugs head toward the light
because the Walrus and Carpenter
told them so

Crime is like an addiction
They love making the legal
illegal
because nothing lives up
to the hype
when it exists
Miracles sold like soap
Laughing more than people realize
because seeing the humor
keeps your brain
from being blown out

The medium is the message
A protest song never delivers a message
only a guitar lick
If you wanna send a message
that bad
use Western Union
All media exists
to reinvent your lives
to something
that you won't be ashamed
to own

Individuality sold
like an Ayn Rand book
that looks good
on the shelves
of wannabe socialists

that never fully grasp
any ideology
Opinions sold for free
by any bald intellectual
that used to rock
the Harry Potter look

Humanity and nature go together
in everything
for we are all everything
an ego in skin
No more and no less
A feature of the whole
so thus
we are the whole

Bruises always heal
in time that always passes
Firepit never goes out
amongst friends
but God help the one
who the smoke wants to follow

A poet of the no collar work force, **Daniel W. Wright** is a mid-western son who loves and loathes the red brick town that surrounds him. A longtime writer of wild nights and whiskey tributes, Wright speaks for the lover in every loner. He is currently the author of six collections of poetry, including *Rodeo of the Soul* (Spartan Press) and *Murder City Special*. His work has appeared in print journals such as *Black Shamrock*, *Gasconade Review*, and *Angel's Share*, underground zines *Bad Jacket* and *Crappy Hour*, and online literary journals such as *Under the Bleachers*, *The Rye Whiskey Review*, and *The Dope Fiend Daily*. He currently resides in St. Louis, MO where you can usually find him in a bar or a bookstore.